W9-AWO-872

Plus 0, Minus 0

Ann H. Matzke

ROURKE
PUBLISHING
www.rourkepublishing.com

www.rourkepublishing.com

PHOTO CREDITS: Cover © Linleo; Titile Page © Cappi Thompason; Page 3 © Chris Scredon, aniravanirav; Page 4,5,6,7 © Ariel Manigsaca; Page 8,9 © aniravanirav; Page 10, 11 © Steve Cole; Page 12, 13 © Chris Scredon; Page 15 © Rmarmion; Page 16, 17, 18 © Rmackay, Greg99; Page 19 © Cappi Thompson; Page 20 © Tony Campbell; Page 21 © James Wimsel; Page 22, 23 © kipuxakipuxa

Edited by Luana Mitten

Cover and Interior design by Teri Intzegian

Library of Congress Cataloging-in-Publication Data

Matzke, Ann
 Plus 0, Minus 0 / Ann Matzke.
    p. cm. -- (Little World Math)
 Includes bibliographical references and index.
 ISBN 978-1-61741-761-0 (hard cover) (alk. paper)
 ISBN 978-1-61741-963-8 (soft cover)
 Library of Congress Control Number: 2011924808

Rourke Publishing
Printed in the United States of America, North Mankato, Minnesota
060711
060711CL

www.rourkepublishing.com - rourke@rourkepublishing.com
Post Office Box 643328 Vero Beach, Florida 32964

Zero means none.

$+ \; 0 \; = \; ?$

Plus zero adds no more.

$- \; 0 \; = \; ?$

Minus zero takes away none.

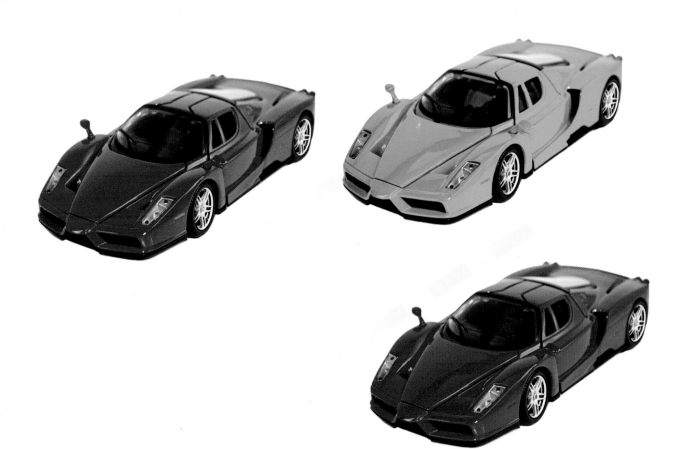

Five cars race.

No more cars join the race.

$$5$$
$$+0$$

$$+ 0 = ?$$

Five cars zoom by.
Adding zero doesn't change the number.

3

4

5

Three umbrellas ready for rain.

Take away zero umbrellas.

$$3$$
$$-0$$
$$\overline{}$$

$$- \; 0 \; = \; ?$$

Raindrops fall, pitter pat.

Taking away zero doesn't change the number.

One soccer ball on the field.

Add zero soccer balls.

$$1 \\ +0 \\ \hline$$

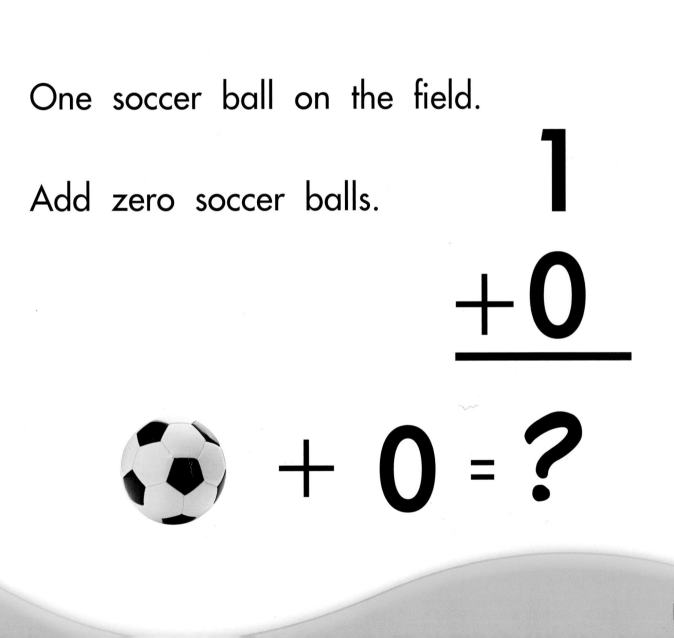 + 0 = ?

One soccer ball kicked from player to player.

Adding zero doesn't change the number.

1

2

Two colorful mittens keep hands warm.

Take away zero mittens.

$$2$$
$$-0$$

 $- 0 =$  ?

Warm hands build a snowman.

Taking away zero doesn't change the number.

Four furry kittens
romp and play.

No more kittens
come this way.

$$4 + 0 - 0 = \text{?}$$

Adding zero doesn't change the number.

A number stays the same when you add zero or take away zero.

Index

Websites

www.ixl.com/math/practice/grade-1-adding-zero

www.ixl.com/math/practice/grade-1-subtracting-0

www.brobstsystems.com/kids/addsheet.htm

About the Author

Ann H. Matzke is a librarian. She lives with her family in the Wild Horse Valley along the old Mormon Trail in Gothenburg, Nebraska. Ann has two dogs and they added two cats to their family. Ann enjoys reading and writing books.